All-Occasion Sentiment Collection

GREETING CARD POETRY FOR YOUR USE

Title Page

Title

All -occasion Sentiment Collection

Subtitle

Greeting card poetry for your use

Author

Lora Brand

Publisher name

Lora Brand

Publisher link

https://doreainspirationspublishings.com.au/books

Copyrights

National Library of Australia cataloguing -in – Publication entry.

Author: Brand, Lora, Author

Editor: van der Merwe. Nadia, Editor

[1] All- Occasion Sentiment Collection

ISBN: 9781763786455

Book Cover by [Lora Brand]

Poetry [Lora Brand]

Contents

Throughout the years I have written poems and gifted them to those around me. The encouragement I received has been overwhelming, with recommendations to compile a book of poetry, to be shared with others.

The impact thoughtful verses have on others has inspired me to publish this book, with the intent of providing others with greetings for their own personal use.

I have often found it difficult to find that right verse for an occasion, which has been my purpose for writing my own. In doing so, I have found much satisfaction and joy as I write.

ACKNOWLEDGEMENTS

Many thanks to my family and friends who have continually encouraged me to write. Your kind words have been the motivation to bring this poetry collection into publication.

Thank you to my editor, Nadia van der Merwe for going above and beyond in assisting me with the completion of this book

Your patience and kindness are very much appreciated.

Baby shower Invitation 1(boy)

First was marriage then the honeymoon,
But wait! Another surprise coming soon.
Inside Mum's belly he now grows,
Right down to his tiny little fingers and toes.
Mysteriously, he knows when it's time to break free.
Out he will come for the world to see.
Here I am! Come make a fuss,
And celebrate me with all of us.

Lora Brand

Baby shower invitation 2 (boy)

Let's get together
and have lots of fun,
For we are soon to give birth to a son
Blue, green, red and yellow,
All the colours for a fine little fellow.
Guess what size? Or colour hair?
Will it be red, dark or rather fair?
Will he be short, chubby, long or slender?
The questions we ask, we now surrender.
The fact remains that we are having a boy,
So please share with us in all our joy.

Lora Brand

Baby shower invitation 3 (girl)

First was marriage then the honeymoon,
But wait! A surprise to be coming soon.
Inside Mum's belly she now grows,
Right down to her tiny little fingers and toes.
Mysteriously she knows when it's time to break free,
Out she will come for the world to see.
Here I am! Come make a fuss,
And celebrate me with all of us.

Lora Brand

Baby shower invitation 4 (girl)

Let's get together
and have loads of laughter,
For soon we will have
a baby daughter.
Purple, pink, rainbow and pearl,
All the colours
for a beautiful girl.
Guess what size? Or colour hair?
Will it be red, dark or rather fair?
Will she be short, chubby, long and slender?
The questions we ask we now surrender.
This little girl we cannot wait to see.
Please share with us
our moment of glee.

Lora Brand

Baby shower congratulations 1

Is it a girl? Is it a boy?
The question is this.
Whatever bub is, they will bring great bliss.
To see the surprise of such a little one,
Yes! You are going
to have so much fun.
That moment of birth
when your eyes make contact,
Overwhelming you with love, that's a fact.
A love so strong
binding you together,
This child is yours forever and ever.

Lora Brand

Baby shower congratulations 2

Will it be a girl?
Will it be a boy?
This will be a surprise
For you to enjoy.

Lora Brand

Baby shower congratulations 3 (boy)

Today we shower you with gifts and joy,
As you await the arrival of your baby boy.
Anticipation of much pleasure,
No comparison by any measure.
Heartfelt joy he will bring,
Far greater than any other thing.
No jewel can compare his priceless worth,
Once he arrives and enters this earth.

One look, one gaze, is all it takes,
Forever change, in your heart, he makes.
No looking back as it was before,
So much joy for you in store.
Not long now he is soon to come,
With many surprises for Dad and Mum.

Best wishes for your future to be,
As you ponder ahead waiting to see.
His eyes – his face – his hair and feet,
For you this is an amazing feat.
Not long now as his birth draws near,
Fulfilling your hearts as you hold him dear.

Lora Brand

Baby shower congratulations 4 (boy)

How precious is
the news I heard,
A baby boy, the scan confirmed.
So much joy he will bring,
Soon challenging everything.
The world you knew
never the same again,
Enhanced with love
and blessings to rain.
Anticipation
captures your heart,
As your new journey
soon to start.
Congratulations
for this joy ahead,
May your days be
with wisdom led.

Lora Brand

Baby shower congratulations 5 (girl)

Pitter patter
of little feet,
Soon to come
for you to meet.
The surprise awaits
for you to see,
Tiny features
on her face to be.
Congratulations
for this bub to come,
Adding to the family
this little one.

Lora Brand

Baby shower congratulations 6 (girl)

How precious is
the news I heard,
A baby girl –
the scan confirmed.
So much joy
she will bring,
Soon changing everything.
The world you knew
never the same again,
Enhanced with love
and blessings to gain.
Anticipation
captures your heart,
As your new journey
soon to start.
Congratulations
for your journey ahead,
May your days be
with wisdom led.

Lora Brand

Baby shower congratulations 7 (girl)

No surprise to you
this one is a girl,
Capturing your heart
as a precious pearl.
Amazing will be the glance
of your first look,
Awaiting to see that breath
she first took.
Nobody can measure
the joy she will bring,
Anticipating to hear
That little voice awakening.
Her day of arrival soon to come,
Changing your name forever to 'Mum'.

Lora Brand

Baby shower congratulations 8 (girl)

Congratulations are in order,
for soon you will have
a baby daughter.
The apple of your eye
she will become,
Your name soon to be Mum.
The most awesome role
in life to play,
Is being a mum day by day.
A jack of all trades
you will become,
With joy and laughter
and many days of fun.

Lora Brand

Baby shower congratulations 9 (girl)

Today we shower you with gifts and laughter,
As you await the arrival of your baby daughter.
Anticipation of the greatest pleasure,
No comparison by any measure.
Heartfelt joy she will bring,
Far greater than any other thing.
No jewel can compare her priceless worth,
Once she arrives and enters this earth.

One look, one gaze, is all it takes,
Forever change, in your heart, she makes.
No looking back as it was before,
For now, much joy for you in store.
Not long now she is soon to come,
With many surprises for Dad and Mum.

Best wishes for your future to be,
As you ponder ahead waiting to see.
Her eyes – her face – her feet- her hair,
Nothing in this world can compare.
Not long now as her birth draws near,
Fulfilling your hearts as you hold her dear.

Lora Brand

Baby shower congratulations 10 (twins)

Twins! Twins! For you it shall be,
Lots of laughter giggles and glee.
Get ready for exciting times to come,
For now, you will be a very busy mum.
The task at hand has been given to you,
Reserved for only just a few.
Overwhelming at times, please don't despair,
Multiplying your joy for they are a pair.
Double trouble – do not believe –
As double blessings you will receive.

Lora Brand

Baby shower congratulations 11 (twin girls)

Two pink dresses, bonnets and bows,
Bright little socks to cover their toes.
Double the treasure that you will receive,
Bonds of love to you they will cleave.

Side by side in the womb they thrive,
Awaiting the day for them to arrive.
Doubling your joy as they are a pair,
Lots of love for you to share.

Awaiting to see the colour of their eyes,
Who they resemble left for surprise.
Black hair, red hair or maybe none,
The anticipation is so much fun.

Their beauty is soon to unfold,
Many tales yet to be told –
Of all the moments that you will treasure,
Creating joy and immense pleasure.

Congratulations as you are soon to expect,
A journey of joy as you truly are blessed.

Lora Brand

Baby shower congratulations 12 (twin girl and boy)

Double blessings soon to come,
For we are two, not just one.
Two hearts to love and give you joy,
One a girl and one a boy.
Loads of washing nappies and feeds,
All part of caring for our needs.
But the reward for you will be immense,
This journey soon to commence.
Oh, the fun, when we begin to play,
Entertaining you day by day.
Laughter, giggles and smiles for you,
As we make each day fresh and new.

Lora Brand

Religious baby shower congratulations 1

A tiny heartbeat
within the womb,
Girl or boy –
we can only presume.
Week by week
growing stronger,
Months pass
now so much longer.
Nose, eyes, ears,
so perfectly designed,
Individually created
as one of a kind.
Soon is the time
for the journey of birth,
What a victory
upon entry to earth.

Lora Brand

Religious baby shower congratulations 2

Congratulations,
parents-to-be,
Will it be a he or maybe a she.
The time of birth
brings a lovely surprise,
Surely joy and tears
will fill your eyes.
A sigh of relief
for the labour that will end,
Bringing many blessings
that God will send.

Lora Brand

Religious baby shower congratulations 3

So many surprises
for you to see,
Is it a he? Or is it a she?
Dark hair, light hair, red hair or none,
The idea of not knowing
is so much fun.
Brown eyes, blue eyes, 'tis all a mystery,
This babe to be born
making new history.
Perfectly formed arms,
legs, feet and hands,
The first breath breathed
as God commands.
Amazing design
coming from the Creator,
Giving much joy, pleasure and laughter.

Lora Brand

Baby birth 1 (from baby's perspective)

Finally, your day has arrived,
For nine months I have thrived.
Hello, Mum! And hello, Dad!
What a journey I've just had.
Safe in your arms I now can rest,
Look at my parents, aren't they the best.
All my needs, you take care of,
In my big world, filled with love.

Lora Brand

Baby birth 2

Nine months' wait
Lookout here I come,
A loud scream!
Where is my mum!
Feed me please
And give me a hug,
Wrap me up tight
Warm and snug.
You may lose sleep
looking after me.
My needs are many
so you see.
But what a joy
I will bring to you,
Smiles and giggles
each day something new.
It might not be easy
looking after me,
But I'm so glad to be
part of this family.

Lora Brand

Baby birth 3 (boy)

At last, your day
finally has come,
You now have
your baby son.
The days ahead
be filled with glee,
Much joy and laughter
for you to see.

Lora Brand

Baby birth 4 (boy)

I heard the best news ever today,
Congratulations is what I have to say.
A job well done for the both of you,
For the birth of this bub, so fresh and new.

Smelling so sweet you could hardly resist,
To give kisses and hugs one must insist.
To nurse this one, he is a treasure,
Giving you always joy and much pleasure.

Lora Brand

Baby birth 5 (boy)

The announcement is out
all said and done,
You are now proud parents
of a healthy son.
May this little man
give much joy and laughter,
For all your days
as well as thereafter.

Lora Brand

Baby birth 6 (boy)

Wrinkly little fingers
wrinkly little toes,
Cute little button
for his nose.
Feet and hands
oh-so small,
Most handsome boy of them all.
How is it possible
to have one so tiny,
Skin so soft
smooth and shiny.
The best gift
you could ever receive,
A baby boy
to which you will cleave.

Lora Brand

Baby birth 7 (boy)

If you could measure love, it must be this,
The birth of your son! Oh, what bliss.
Instant overwhelming feelings from within,
When your eyes connect with your brand-new kin.
No words to explain the emotions of joy,
As you now hold your new baby boy.
A love so pure from that one instant gaze,
A heart of love now set ablaze.

Lora Brand

Baby birth 8 (boy)

Congrats, congrats,
For a job well done!
For the safe arrival,
Of your little son.

Lora Brand

Baby birth 9 (boy)

Congratulations for your new bambino,
Far greater than winning lottery or keno
For this little gift will be yours forever,
Outweighing any earthly treasure.

To train – to love – embrace and to hold,
Cannot be compared to silver or gold.
A bond so strong with great reward,
Together, many adventures to be explored.

Lora Brand

Baby birth 10 (nephew)

We are very excited as our nephew has arrived,
Emerging from his cocoon, where he thrived.
A new addition in our lives – we are blessed,
A baby boy, we could not have guessed.
Uncle and Aunty, the proudest of kin,
Much to be embraced as your life will now begin.
Tiny, adorable and wonderful are you,
Radiance of a sunset, you will outdo,
To us you are a precious joy,
Our nephew and beautiful baby boy.

Congratulations, Mum and Dad, for a job well done,
Shining love in your hearts brighter than the sun.

Lora Brand

Baby birth 11 (twin boys)

Baby boys, you now have two,
What to expect this next year through.
Playmates to begin their very first years,
Joyful moments with many happy tears.

Double the washing, double the mess,
Double the chores for you to address.
Double the smiles and giggles you get,
Double the surprises to come as yet.

Watching them grow will be a great pleasure,
A household of love, way beyond measure.
The joy these two will bring to your heart,
A love yearning never to be apart.

Their personalities will differ, of that I'm sure,
Increasing your delight and much, much more.
Far more than gold or a trophy they be,
creating many treasured moments, you see.

Congratulations on the birth of these two,
As your lives now unfold anew.

Lora Brand

Firstborn baby birth 12 (boy)

It's a boy and already a heavy weight,
Hoping to be Daddy's new fishing mate.
A handsome strong little dude is he,
No longer two but a family of three.

A fine young man he will surely grow,
Wherever Daddy be, he is sure to go.
Ready to learn from boy to man,
To be like his dad as quick as he can.

And like Mummy too for she is the best,
And in raising a son, she is truly blessed.

Lora Brand

Baby birth with siblings 13 (boy)

Today you are given a baby boy,
Enriching your lives, giving you much joy.
Precious is this little one,
Now, at last, you have a son.
Enlarging your family, oh, what a treat!
The pitter patter of little feet.
Laughter and giggles soon to follow,
As your little man will quickly grow.
Enjoy each day as it unfolds,
With many a joyous time life holds.
Congratulations to the both of you,
And special mention to the other siblings too.
Adding to your family such a great pleasure,
You could never count or even measure.

Lora Brand

Baby birth 14 (girl)

Congratulations to you: Mum and Dad,
For this precious little gift you both just had.
Ribbons and bows this little one is a she,
In pink, she is and pretty she will always be.
A wardrobe full, of glamour and glitz,
With fashion accessories and all those bits.
A baby girl to teach and to raise,
With lots of love and many a praise.
A princess in your eyes, to behold,
Many a joyful time yet to unfold.
Patience and love will be the key,
In nurturing all she is to be.

Lora Brand

Baby birth 15 (girl)

I heard the best news ever today,
Congratulations is what I have to say.
A job well done for the both of you,
For the birth of this bub so fresh and new.

Smelling so sweet you could hardly resist,
To give kisses and cuddles one must insist,
To nurse this one for she is a treasure,
Giving you always joy and much pleasure.

Lora Brand

Baby birth 16 (girl)

There is now a love that never ever wanes,
You have a daughter – this fact remains –
A baby girl for you to nurture and protect,
The art of parenthood for you to perfect.
There may be tears, some mess, and learning for you,
Days full of adventures and much more to do.
But the best days unfold one by one,
As your journey together has now begun.

Lora Brand

Baby birth 17 (girl)

Wrinkly little fingers,
wrinkly little toes,
Cute little button
for her nose.
Her feet and hands
oh-so small,
Most gorgeous girl
of them all.
How is it possible
to have one so tiny?
Skin so soft,
smooth and shiny.
The best gift
you could ever receive,
A baby girl
to which you will cleave.

Lora Brand

Baby birth 18 (girl)

If you could measure love, it must be this,
The birth of your daughter! Oh, what bliss.
Instant overwhelming feelings from within,
When your eyes connect with your brand-new kin.
No words to explain, your heart's in a whirl,
As you now hold your baby girl.
A love so pure from that one instant gaze,
A heart of love now set ablaze.

Lora Brand

Baby birth 19 (girl)

Congratulations for your new bambina,
More valuable is she, than gold or silver
For this little gift will be yours forever,
Outweighing any earthly treasure.

To train – to love – embrace and to hold,
Cannot be compared to silver or gold.
A bond so strong with great reward,
Together, many adventures to be explored.

Lora Brand

Baby birth 20 (niece)

We are very excited as our niece has arrived,
Emerging from her cocoon, where she thrived.
A new addition in our lives – we are blessed,
A baby girl, we could not have guessed.
Uncle and Aunty, the proudest of kin,
Much to be embraced as your life will now begin.
Tiny, adorable and wonderful are you,
Radiance of a sunset, you will outdo,
To us you are a precious pearl,
Our niece and beautiful baby girl.

Congratulations, Mum and Dad, for a job well done,
Shining love in your hearts brighter than the sun.

Lora Brand

Baby birth 21 (twin girls)

Finally, the day
for your girls to be here,
Hip, hip, hooray!
Congratulations and cheer.
Marking your calendar
in a special way,
As each year now commemorates
a double birthday.
The cutest of all,
the two bubs be,
Proudly arrived
for the world to see.
Amazingly created
in every way,
Now, they are yours
and here to stay.
Their hands and feet
and sweet tiny faces,
Already showing off
their little airs and graces.
All colours of a rainbow
these two can wear,
Parading a show
of an adorable pair.
All the best wishes
for your future ahead,
May you, as parents,
with wisdom, be led.

Lora Brand

Religious baby birth 1

Who could possibly design
something so great,
'Tis more than chance or simply fate.
So perfectly formed in every way,
This baby growing day by day.
A baby given to you to nurture,
Also, for you
much joy and pleasure.
Trust in the Designer
for the task ahead,
For help comes
in His Word, it is said.

Lora Brand

Religious baby birth 2 (boy)

What a surprise! What a joy,
You now have a baby boy.
Congratulations to you, Mum and Dad,
Now to name your little lad.

His tiny hands and wrinkly feet,
Oh, the joy, when you first meet.
Perfectly formed and handsome is he,
As you hold him up for all to see.

Nothing compares to what this gift will bring.
In your hearts you will surely sing,
A song of joy! A song of love!
As this gift comes truly from above.

A master's design is what you see,
A magnificent Creator surely is He.

Lora Brand

Religious baby birth 3 (boy)

Distinct features upon his face,
Designed by God in all His grace.
Perfectly formed
in every way,
Truly God's splendour on display.
A brand-new life
entrusted in your care,
A bond of love
together you will share,
Trust in God
for the wisdom you will need,
With his instruction manual
please take heed.
For this little one
depends entirely on you,
For teaching and training
all his years through.

Lora Brand

Religious baby birth 4 (boy)

Expecting soon a little man,
Another to join the family clan.
May this one be handsome and strong,
To your hearts he shall belong.
A boy that has wisdom strength and love,
Given directly from the Father above.
With eyes that see beyond his years,
A heart of peace having no fears.

Lora Brand

Religious baby birth 5 (boy)

Did you ever get such a surprise,
Catching that glimpse with your eyes,
Of your new baby boy born to you,
Skin so soft and ever so new.

To hold that one in your arms of love,
A precious gift from the Father above.
A designed brand and unique too,
Formed and fashioned to be like you.

Hands so tiny, face so small,
Oh! The cutest of them all.
Complete in every possible way,
Congratulations is what I say.

Lora Brand

Religious baby birth 6 (girl)

Did you ever get such a surprise,
Catching that glimpse with your eyes.
Of your new baby girl born to you,
Skin so soft and ever so new.

To hold that one in your arms of love,
A precious gift from the Father above.
A designed brand and unique too,
Formed and fashioned to be like you.

Hands so tiny, face so small,
Oh! The cutest of them all.
Complete in every possible way,
Congratulations is what I say.

Lora Brand

Religious baby birth 7 (girl)

Distinct features upon her face,
Designed by God in all His grace.
Perfectly formed
in every way,
Truly God's splendour on display.
A brand-new life
entrusted in your care,
A bond of love
together you will share.
Trust in God
for the wisdom you will need,
With his instruction manual
please take heed.
For this little one
depends entirely on you,
For teaching and training
all her years through.

Lora Brand

General 1-year-old birthday 1

Sweets and cake to fill your tum,
What a treat as you turn one.
Colourful balloons and delightful decorations,
Wishing you the best for your birthday celebrations.

Lora Brand

General 1-year-old birthday 2

Congratulations you are one today,
A party for you with a fun-filled day!
Cake enjoyed as it passes your lips,
Delightedly clutched with your fingertips.
A day of kisses and hugs to the end,
With our birthday wishes to you we send.

Lora Brand

1-year-old birthday 3 (boy)

A handsome prince now turns one,
Hope your day is filled with fun!
One candle, one cake, plus more to eat,
To give your tummy a tasty treat.

Presents, surprises from family and friends,
You might wish this day never ends.
Many hugs and kisses outweigh them all,
Too cute to refuse one so small.

Run and play and use all your might,
Then to bed, to sleep well at night.
Dreaming dreams of the birthday just had,
'Twas such a big day for a tiny little lad.

Lora Brand

1-year-old birthday 4 (girl)

A gorgeous princess now turns one,
Hope your day is filled with fun!
One candle, one cake plus more to eat,
To give your tummy a tasty treat.
Presents and surprises from family and friends,
Making you wish this day never ends.
Many hugs and kisses outweigh them all,
Too cute to refuse one so small.
Run and play using all your might,
Then to bed to sleep well at night.
Dreaming dreams of all that came your way,
Celebrating, this joy, your first birthday.

Lora Brand

General 2-year-old birthday 1

First there was one year and now there are two,
You've grown so big! What will we do?
Once you couldn't talk and now you say a lot,
From a tiny bub to a little tot.

You are so much fun and we love you heaps,
With many memories in our hearts for keeps.
Funny things you say and do are priceless to us,
No wonder we make such a big fuss.

A big birthday wish, with love and cheer,
As now you will begin a brand-new year.

Lora Brand

General 2-year-old birthday 2

Oh, what fun
you will have this day.
Birthday cake
with a hip, hip, hooray!
Family and friends
to celebrate with you,
For now, you turn a tiny two.

Lora Brand

2-year-old birthday (boy)

Oh, what fun you will have this day,
Birthday cake with a hip, hip, hooray!
Family and friends to celebrate with you,
For now, you turn a tiny two.

First you arrived as loud as can be,
Then we saw you – a handsome he.
Sleep and eat you did lots,
Now you have joined the clan of tots.

Running here, there and everywhere,
Wherever your eyes fixed you would care.
'Terrible twos' they say – not true,
As you learn what is not for you.

Some days are tricky, being a little man,
So have loads of fun, as much as you can.
Enjoy your birthday with lots of cheer,
May your family be with you close and near.

Lora Brand

2-year-old birthday (girl)

Oh, what fun you will have this day,
Birthday cake with a hip, hip, hooray!
Family and friends to celebrate with you,
For now, you turn a tiny two.

First you arrived as loud as can be,
Then we saw you, a precious little she.
Sleep and eat you did lots,
Now you have joined the clan of tots.

Running here there and everywhere,
Wherever your eyes fixed you would care.
Terrible twos, they say – not true,
As you learn what is not for you.

Some days are tricky being a little girl,
So, laugh, play and dance with a twirl.
Enjoy your birthday with loads of cheer,
May your family be with you close and near.

Lora Brand

General 3-year-old birthday

Three years,
Three wishes
for you to make,
Not to mention
a birthday cake.
A little character
you have become,
Such a delight
for Dad and Mum.
A curious mind
taking in all,
Who could resist
one so small.
With that cute
little smile
and cheeky grin,
Kisses for you
Over and over again.

Lora Brand

General 4-year-old birthday

Now you are four, growing up so fast,
How the months and years
have quickly passed.
Still as cute as ever could be,
With eyes that sparkle
With cheek and glee.

Lora Brand

General 5-year-old birthday

A happy day for you
as you now turn five,
Get down and boogie
and do that jive.
Fun and laughter
to fill your day,
Let's give you a big
hip, hip, hooray!

Lora Brand

5-year-old birthday (girl)

The most precious girl turns five today,
Eyes full of excitement to begin her day.
What surprises will your birthday bring,
Causing you to laugh, dance and sing.

A joyful little girl you are to us,
And, so, for you we make a fuss.
Five kisses for you on your cheek,
And many more throughout the week.

Have the best birthday you could ever get,
One you will remember and never forget.
We love you so much, darling, we say,
So, hope you have the best ever day.

Lora Brand

General 6-year-old birthday 1

A big birthday wish
for you today,
Six years ago, you arrived
on this special day.
A day that we
will always remember,
For in our hearts
you are a treasure.

Lora Brand

General 6-year-old birthday 2

Six today!
What an exciting day!
Party, fun,
and friends to play.
With hugs and gifts
'Best wishes,' we say,
Celebrating you
on this, your birthday!

Lora Brand

6-year-old birthday 1 (boy)

Six years ago, you came to earth,
A character you've been since your birth.
To watch you grow has been a pleasure,
For you truly are a little treasure.
From baby to boy growing up so fast,
How the years have quickly passed.
May this birthday be the best you have had,
Giving joy to you, a special little lad.

Lora Brand

6-year-old birthday 2 (boy)

For a delightful little boy
who now turns six.
Spritely and joyful
and often full of tricks.
To us you are the apple of our eyes,
Each day giving many a surprise.
The joy you bring
each day new,
May it be returned
doubly back to you.

Happy Birthday!

Lora Brand

6-year-old birthday (girl)

Six today!
What an exciting day!
Party, fun,
and friends to play.
With hugs and gifts
'Best wishes,' we say,
Celebrating you
on this, your birthday!

Happy Birthday!

Lora Brand

General 7-year-old birthday

Seven is the age you turn today,
Many surprises to come your way.
All our love with you we celebrate,
On your birthday, this special date.
May you have the best day ever,
Making the day last forever.

Lora Brand

7-year-old birthday 1 (boy)

A big happy birthday
to a boy turning seven,
Hugs and kisses raining
down from heaven.
What special treats will come your way?
As all fun unfolds on your special day.
Will there be lollies
presents and surprise,
From the moment you wake
and open your eyes?
I say, yes, and much, much more,
For you today there is lots in store.

Lora Brand

7-year-old birthday 2 (boy)

Seven today,
A great age to be,
The wonders of life
for you to see.
Imaginations and
mysteries yet to unfold,
Many great stories
not yet told –
Of heroes, villains
princesses and kings,
Of land and sea
and all kinds of things,
Of a birthday boy
and the day ahead,
Till evening comes
and you rest your head.

Lora Brand

7-year-old birthday 1 (girl)

A big happy birthday
to a girl turning seven,
Hugs and kisses
raining down from heaven.
What special treats will come your way,
As the day unfolds on your birthday.
Will there be lollies
presents and a surprise?
From the moment you wake
and open your eyes.
I say yes, and much, much more
For you today there is lots in store.

Lora Brand

7-year-old birthday 2 (girl)

Seven today –
a great age to be,
The wonders of life
for you to see.
Imaginations and
mysteries yet to unfold,
Many great stories
Not yet told,
Of heroes, villains
princesses and kings,
Of land and sea
and all kinds of things,
Of a birthday adventure
and the day ahead,
Till evening comes
and you rest your head.

Lora Brand

General 8-year-old birthday

Today you are turning eight,
Let's get together and celebrate!
With fun and games and a party treat,
Delicious food for all to eat.
Bring loads of laughter, joy and tears,
Hip, hip, hooray! Ringing in our ears.
What a joy! What a surprise!
Unfolding before all our eyes.
Do not be late nor hesitate,
To celebrate this party date.

Lora Brand

8-year-old birthday (boy)

Daddy's little fishing mate,
Has now turned a big eight.
Away with all the fishing toys,
A rod now for bigger boys.
Time to catch the biggest of fish,
To be served as the dinner dish.
Growing up fast is our young man,
Taking in all as quick as you can.
The years ahead for you to explore,
Many fun times for you in store.

Lora Brand

8-year-old birthday (daughter)

Daddy's little girl now turning eight,
His princess ready for a party date.
Frills and bows with a pretty dress,
For you, my sweetie, nothing less.
A birthday wish I give to you,
With all my love and kisses too.

Lora Brand

General 9-year-old birthday 1

Nine! Nine!
What an age to be.
Happy birthday
to you we decree.
Nine hugs and kisses
to celebrate your day,
With gifts and surprises
coming your way.
Nine years of love
on you it rains,
As you are dear to us
this fact remains.
Our love for you
is far beyond measure,
For you truly are
our special treasure.

Lora Brand

General 9-year-old birthday 2

Nine a great age for you to be,
More to explore, a whole world to see.
A curious mind of everything around,
The wonders of life yet to be found.

Discoveries and colours of every shade,
With lasting memories yet to be made.
Animals, plants, the earth and the beach,
Exploration of all within your reach.
Much to take in for one who is nine,
Best to enjoy one day at a time.

As nine best wishes your birthday brings,
And the year ahead many new things.

Lora Brand

9-year-old birthday (boy)

To be nine is a great
and wonderful joy,
Especially
when you are a boy.
There is much to love
throughout this year,
Have a great birthday
with loads of cheer.

Lora Brand

9-year-old birthday (daughter)

To a beautiful daughter
who now turns nine,
Funny and witty
and mighty fine.
Not a baby nor a teenager
just a little in between,
With the most delightful eyes
you have ever seen.
A character of joy
you are to us,
So of course, for you
we make a fuss.
In hoping to give you
the best birthday ever,
One for you
to always remember.
Happy birthday, sweetheart,
this day is for you,
With all our love
and best wishes too.

Lora Brand

10-year-old birthday (girl)

Ten is a cool
age to be,
What's in store
is for you to see.
Music, dancing
playing in the sun,
For all to join
in your birthday fun.
A sleepover to be
your ultimate dream,
Bringing to your eyes
a joyful gleam.
Surprising you
with a gift or two,
This day is special
and all about you.

Lora Brand

General 10-year-old birthday

Double figures you have now reached – ten,
Birthdays keep coming again and again.
What will this one bring about,
Let's begin with a birthday shout!

Family and friends to celebrate with you,
A present, a surprise or even two,
Make your first wish by closing your eyes,
With hope and expectations beginning to rise.

May this day be one of your best,
Full of excitement, zeal and zest!

Lora Brand

General16-year-old birthday

May the best wishes come as you turn sixteen,
More than you've known or ever seen.
May life surprise you with many an unknown,
Beyond imagination of all you've been shown.

A treasury of love surrounding your heart,
Gifts and surprises beginning from the start,
Of your next years prior to twenty-one,
A full measure of life second to none.

Enjoy the age you have reached this day,
Many happy returns to come your way.

Lora Brand

Teenage birthday

A teenager now – oh wow – lookout,
Hooray! Let's give a birthday shout.
Highs and lows of the next years to remain,
Parents thinking they're going insane.

Not a child nor an adult, it's those years in between,
Developing character and maturity often unseen.
The imaginations of life exploding much to explore,
Temptation presenting itself hard to ignore.

The best years of life ahead of you yet,
Possibilities and dreams forming your mindset.
Shaping your character for your future to be,
As far as your eyes could possibly see.

Wishing you all the best as you navigate the next years,
Happy birthday to you and a big three cheers!

Lora Brand

21-year-old birthday (male)

Twenty-one today is the birthday guy,
Time to celebrate and reach the sky.
May this day bring many a surprise,
Unfolding much before your eyes.
Much love, much joy your future to bring,
Far greater than any other thing.
The world ahead is at your feet,
Many new friends for you to meet.
Grasp every opportunity that comes your way,
Seizing each moment day by day.
For you, I wish years of joy ahead,
May your life be rich and wisdom led.

Lora Brand

21-year-old birthday (female)

Twenty-one today is the birthday girl,
Precious you are as a priceless pearl.
May this day bring many a surprise,
Unfolding much before your eyes.
Much love, much joy your future to bring,
Far greater than any diamond ring.
The world ahead is at your feet,
Many new friends for you to meet.
Grasp every opportunity that comes your way,
Seizing each moment day by day.
For you, I wish years of joy ahead,
May your life be rich and wisdom led.

Lora Brand

Senior birthday 1

It's not the question of age that counts,
But the love you gave in huge amounts,
The previous years of a life you shared,
The ways in which you truly cared.

Those years behind making great history,
A solid foundation built in a strong family,
Many memories in your heart always to behold,
A heritage of love yet to unfold.

Many years you have lived, much wisdom you've gained,
As each year passed by, your steadfastness remained,
A treasure box of wealth you richly taught,
Not monetary value, but lessons caught.

Of a life well lived throughout your days,
Seeing many celebrations on your birthdays.
Another now has arrived again,
Showering on you love, as sweet-smelling rain.

Happy birthday!

Lora Brand

Senior birthday 2

A lifetime of blood, sweat and tears,
As you leave behind your younger years.
Your journey is yet to see life at its best,
Wisdom and knowledge gained; you have passed the test.

This brings maturity which of course is priceless,
In a rich full measure making you precious.
Faith, love and hope are what remains,
Far outweighing any of the richest gains.

May this birthday be to you all it can be,
Giving you more joy in life you could ever see,
Rich in love and blessings all year through,
As I send this birthday wish to you.

Lora Brand

General Birthday 1

Happy birthday,
Happy birthday,
Happy birthday,
Many great blessings
to come your way!
May today bring you
joy and laughter,
Not only today
but many days after.

Lora Brand

General Birthday 2

Party! Party!
Party for you,
Another year
to start brand new.
Birthday celebrations
have come your way,
For this being
your very special day.

Lora Brand

General Birthday 3

Today is
your special day,
Happy birthday to you
is what I say.
A day full of surprises,
may it be,
Bringing joy and laughter
and lots of glee.
A present or two
will not go amiss,
As from me I send
a hug and a kiss –
To last your
special day through
And continue on
the next year too.

Lora Brand

General Birthday 4

Hope this birthday
gives you many a surprise,
With joy and laughter
gleaming through your eyes.
All the fun and love
this world may bring,
And in your heart a song
you will sing.

Lora Brand

General Birthday 5

Each year
you are a little older,
Becoming brave
and much bolder.
Experiencing new things
day by day,
Many surprises
coming your way.
May this birthday
bring to you,
Many new things
to see and do.
With loads of love,
laughter and cheer,
To carry on throughout
all this year.

Lora Brand

Birthday (boy) 1

Happy Birthday
to our special little man,
Hope you have as much fun
as you possibly can.
A day filled with laughter
and lots of cheer,
As in our hearts
you are very dear.

Lora Brand

Birthday (boy) 2

A birthday wish
for a fine
young lad,
May this be
the best one
you've ever had.

Lora Brand

Birthday (boy) 3

I heard a young man
celebrates his birthday today,
Love and best wishes
is what I say.
May your day
be more
than
you would
expect,
With pressies
and hugs
and kisses
to collect.

Lora Brand

Birthday (girl) 1

Butterflies, bows
and pretty things,
Princes and princesses
queens and kings.
Imaginations and dreams
a young girl sees.
What's in store?
Oh, tell me please!
As your birthday arrives
you look around,
Not a word, not a whisper
not even a sound.
Then a big loud cheer
and a hip, hip, hooray!
As we all shout
Happy Birthday!

Lora Brand

Birthday (girl) 2

Cupcakes, cupcakes,
everywhere,
All the treats and much fanfare.
A birthday feast
for you it's true,
As well as friends
and family too.
A day of celebration
party and cheer,
For in our hearts
you are so dear.
May today bring you joy
and much pleasure,
Making memories
that you'll always treasure.

Lora Brand

Birthday (male) 1

What would
a bloke
wish for
on his birthday,
Let's just leave it at that
not a word to say.
A day
to remember,
a day
of good cheer,
This one's on me
so here is a beer.

Lora Brand

Birthday (male) 2

Birthday equals cake
and possibly one wish,
One warning I give
as you consider this.
The one wish you ask for
may possibly come true,
Could also last
the whole year through.

So, give it much thought
before you make your request,
As one would hope
this will make your life blessed.
A wish to remember
and one that will last,
Allowing your year
to begin with a blast.

Lora Brand

Birthday (male) 3

Happy
Birthday,
bloke.
Have a good
one.

Lora Brand

Birthday (female) 1

A birthday wish to you I send,
Love and hugs till your day's end.
Thinking of you wishing I could be there,
Together this day we could share.

Instead, I send all my best wishes,
Of chocolates divine and so delicious,
A birthday full without measure,
As one would find with buried treasure.

Enjoy your day with all it holds,
And all the surprises this day unfolds.
Happy birthday to you – hope all is well,
Many blessing to come as far as the eye can tell.

Lora Brand

Birthday (female) 2

Another birthday
showers on you today.
May it be filled
with love
in a beautiful array –
Of flowers
and friends
to celebrate with you,
Laughter and joy
all the day through.

Happy Birthday

Lora Brand

Father's Day 1

Dad, I love you.
Dad you are mine.
Dad you are awesome.
Dad you're just fine.

Lora Brand

Father's Day 2

Today is the time to say my dad is the greatest,
With kisses and hugs that are the best.
You take my hand when I am afraid,
When I am sick you come to my aid.
When I fall down you help me out,
Thank you, Dad, I now will shout:
Happy Dad's Day to you all day,
With fun and games for us to play.

Lora Brand

Father's Day 3

A hole in one
is no surprise,
Dad, you're a champion
in my eyes.
One who fixes
his eye on the game,
One goal in mind
to be your aim.
Steadfast and sturdy
this always true,
So happy Father's Day
to a fantastic you.

Lora Brand

Father's Day 4

Dad, I honour you
this very day,
For making me special
in every way.
Your provision
your love and endless supply,
An amazing dad
you are that guy.
You taught me love
honour and respect,
Demonstrating life and courage
has an everlasting effect.
Leading me in all
my young years through,
From baby to teenager
and into maturity too.
Thanks, Dad,
have an awesome day.
I appreciate you,
I am proud to say.

Lora Brand

Father's Day 5

Cheers, Dad,
for today
is your day.
So, relax
and enjoy
in every
possible way.

Lora Brand

Father's Day (son)

The best fish
you ever caught,
Can never be sold
nor was ever bought.
It's me, Dad, your awesome son,
Of course, I am your number one.
Thank you for bringing
out the best in me,
Your prize, your joy
for all to see.
I love you, Dad,
with all my heart.
Thank you for all
you do impart.

Lora Brand

Father's Day (daughter)

The best fish
you ever caught,
Can never be sold
nor was ever bought.
It's me, Dad! Your princess,
your queen,
The best catch
you've ever seen.
Thank you for bringing
out the best in me,
Your prize, your joy
for all to see.
I love you, Dad,
with all my heart
Thank you for all
you do impart.

Lora Brand

Mother's Day 1

How many people
have a mum like you,
Whose love and care
Shone each day through.
The grooviest mum
with a flair for fashion,
Seizing life with zeal
laughter and passion.
A mum who is always
true to her name,
As her family comes first,
her love will remain.

Lora Brand

Mother's Day 2

Mum, you are absolutely the best,
Sassy, charming
and full of zest.
Always ready to help in need,
The most awesome mum
you are indeed.
Loving and caring
in every way,
Giving of your love
each new day.
Like a rainbow, you shine
in my heart,
Always close,
never too far apart.
Mum, you are my rock
and solid foundation.
I love you forever
with all my admiration.

Lora Brand

Mother's Day 3

May today be all you hope it to be,
With your family around for you to see.
Honour and praise to you I give,
For was you who gave me life to live.

Thank you for the secrets to life you taught,
Could only be learned, not sold or bought.
You selflessly gave all that you could,
To make my life especially good.

Those values I have were modelled from you,
Always finding ways to see each day through.
So, a big thank you and many blessings to come,
For who you are and for being my mum.

Lora Brand

Mother's Day (from 'us') 4

Mum, you are absolutely the best,
Sassy, charming
and full of zest.
Always ready to help in need,
The most awesome mum
you are indeed.
Loving and caring
in every way,
Giving us your love
each new day.
Like a rainbow you shine
in our heart,
Always close
never too far apart.
Mum, you are our rock
and solid foundation.
We love you forever
with all our admiration.

Lora Brand

Mother's Day (from 'us') 5

May today be all you hope it to be,
With your family around for you to see,
Honour and praise to you we give,
For was you who gave us life to live.

Thank you for the secrets in life you taught,
Could only be learned not sold or bought.
You selflessly gave all that you could,
To make our lives especially good.

Those values we have were modelled from you,
Always finding ways to see each day through.
So, a big thank you and many blessings to come,
For who you are and for being our mum.

Lora Brand

Mother

A mother is one who loves you since birth,
Preparing you for your life here on earth.
A little discipline would never go astray,
This is for your good often she would say.

If you fell down, a mother would be there,
With kisses and hugs, her love to share.
Often other siblings to care for as well,
And yes, I am sure many a story to tell.

Amazing are mothers with many jobs they do,
Chef, event planner, coach just to name a few.
Then to referee brothers and sisters at times,
As arguments fill the air, melodiously like chimes.

Keeping everyone cared for is the goal in mind,
Then at last some rest for herself to find.
The end of each day to lay down her head,
Thinking once more of the day that's ahead.

Lora Brand

Friends

Friends are the people we become,
Many memories made, and then some.
Diverse in thoughts, ideas and ways,
Indifference will not easily faze.
Friends are a valuable treasure,
Unity and care knitting souls together.
Forgiveness and love go hand in hand,
As friendships grow and take a stand.
Layer upon layer as bricks in a wall,
Friends remain through it all.

So glad I have a friend in you,
enriching my life each year through.

Lora Brand

Engagement congratulations

Two hearts beat a rhythm, song and a dance,
The beginning of a beautiful romance.
Growing together in a melody of love,
Entwined as one like a hand to a glove.
The time has come as love has grown deep,
Enhancing this rhythm with a commitment to keep.
An engagement has now been said,
With the betrothal of two soon to be wed.
Congratulations and best wishes for your journey together,
May this rhythm and dance be in your hearts forever.

Lora Brand

Wedding invitation (from child's perspective)

Come celebrate with Dad, Mum and me,
Simply a wedding shall it be.
………. – mark on your calendar,
Our special day for you to remember.

A long time coming this decision to make,
Proud of Dad and Mum and this step they take –
Of a journey together to live day by day,
Filled with hopes and dreams along the way.

First there were two and later came me,
The best part of my special family.
Together in love, we will do our best,
To ensure this day is great, for you, our guest.

A wishing well for your convenience,
Please don't go to much expense.
Simply join us and witness our day,
Finishing with fun, party and play.

Lora Brand

Wedding (wishing well)

………………. & ……………. appreciate your thought,
Of housewares, linen and gifts to be bought.
Some of these things we previously required,
Now thanks to many there is much we've acquired.
Your time may be limited to shop and look around,
Possibly hours passed, yet no gift to be found.
Also to avoid disappointment of two of a kind,
You may prefer a monetary gift – we really don't mind.
A wishing well will be provided for you,
Accommodating this, envelopes too.
Looking forward to you celebrating with us together,
As we begin sharing our lives forever.

Lora Brand

Wedding congratulations 1

Forever changed, your lives will start,
As two loves become one heart.
One heart to plan your lives ahead,
One heart together each day be led.
One heart to blossom a sweet romance,
One heart entwined as a beautiful dance.
Together forever your journey is said,
As today you both, in love, be wed.

Lora Brand

Wedding congratulations 2

One look! One gaze! That's all it took,
Two hearts caught as on a fishing hook.
Lured to one another as a strong current,
And swept together to form one torrent.
Passion growing deep in their heart,
Never the same two lives now start.
A new beginning is what lies ahead,
As two now enter marriage and be wed.
To build a life with memories to come,
For the two now joined together as one.
Congratulations and best wishes I give,
May many long years together you live.

Lora Brand

Religious wedding congratulations 1

A treasure in one another you both have found,
Far greater than rubies, gold, or any gem around.
A treasure of love cannot be bought or sold,
An adornment of beauty for your eyes to behold.

Master jewellers you now have become,
As you shape this treasure together as one.
A diamond is cut to bring out all its glory,
As it is with love, now begins this story.

The jeweller polishes and shows off their prize,
Transforming its beauty before one's eyes.
As a husband cherishes and honours his bride,
She will be a glistening ornament by his side.

Her beauty enhanced by his admiration and love,
Peace in her heart descending as a dove.
As a jeweller he protects and nurtures his find,
Glistening with joy, she is one of a kind.

In response, she will be the fulfillment of his desire,
As his love will be the fuel for his passion and fire.
He captures her heart with every loving glance,
Caressing her with his sweet romance.

Forever changing, her love will grow,
As that priceless gem has beauty to show.
Now for her to be a jeweller as well,
Captivating his heart for all to tell.

To appreciate, to honour, to respect and to love,
Always the plan from the Father above.
Proud, tall and strong, by her side,
The word of God to be their guide

She can trust the decisions that he will make,
For she knows his concern for her is at stake.
She presents him well in the public view,
Admired by many, not just a few.

Refined as gold awaiting his praise,
As she looks at him with that lasting gaze.
Complimenting him in their journey together,
A lifelong love to last forever.

Lora Brand

Religious wedding congratulations (personalised)

What a blessing to find true love,
'Tis really a gift from Father above.
For …………… and …………….. a joy to behold,
As the journey together continues to unfold.
And be joined as one – two hearts shall be,
……………… as well, making it three.
The fulfillment of hopes and dreams to aspire,
Fuelled by love, passion and fire.
My joy for you both nothing can compare,
As I see the love you both have to share.
I pray the very best wishes for you,
Many happy days and prosperity too.
I can truly say I am proud of you today,
To see you both come together this way.
For you …………….. my greatest joy,
Awaited the day that you met this boy.
For you ……………… a delight to see,
A warm welcome into our family.

Lora Brand

Easter 1

This Easter may you
be richly blessed,
With chocolates and sweets
that are divinely best.
Some chocolate
that brings flavour
of an amazing kind,
One that will surely
blow your mind.
A flower or two
would not go amiss,
To bless your day
I am sure of this.
May this Easter bring
you loads of pleasure,
One to remember
and always
to treasure.

Lora Brand

Easter 2

May this Easter
bring you
much pleasure and delight,
With chocolates
and sweets
so many in sight.
Some family fun
to add to this season,
Bringing love and joy
into completion.
Enjoy this Easter
with some time to rest,
May you and yours be
richly blessed.

Happy Easter!

Lora Brand

Religious Easter 1

Easter tells a story of one who did die,
Three days in the grave He would lie.
Buried with Him lies our sin and shame.
Taking on Himself all our blame.

Trading His life for our freedom to gain,
Eternally forever our lives to remain.
What more could one hope for or possibly desire,
Purifying us with His Holy fire.

This Easter, may it be that in all He has done,
Your life remains forever with God's Son.
Happy Easter with best wishes and all His love,
With richest blessings from Father above.

Lora Brand

Religious Easter 2

It's not the eggs, chocolates and more,
'Tis about this season opening a door,
Of new life – of hope and a reason to live,
Of all the freedom His life did give.

To be born as one who would trade our place,
Carrying our load with His amazing grace,
A fierce battle as He was sentenced to die,
Facing death with love – no ordinary guy.

'Father, forgive them for they know not what they do,'
His last prayer uttered for God's plan He knew.
In death He took all the wrongs we've done,
Erasing them each one by one.

'It is finished,' said He before His body hung dead,
All is now forgiven – nothing left unsaid.
Arise now with new life in Him,
Daring to hope and believe again.

Lora Brand

Christmas 1

Christmas fun, Christmas cheer,
Christmas ushering in a new year.
May this be one always to remember,
Carrying you through to next December.

Lora Brand

Christmas 2

Love and cheer I send to you,
To last this Christmas season through.
Of laughter, joy, family and friends,
Sharing together till this season ends.

Happy Christmas and have a great year,
May it be full of fun and cheer.

Lora Brand

Religious Christmas 1 (family)

Happy Christmas to my family I love,
Many blessings on you poured out from above.
May this Christmas bring many a surprise,
Causing joy and laughter to your eyes.

Lora Brand

Religious Christmas 2

Carols, presents, the surprise is near,
For everywhere you look Christmas is here.
A season for family, friendship and love,
This all comes from the Father above.

The plan was God's, a day of celebration,
To honour Jesus, His very own son,
Then to share Him with all mankind,
A plan of redemption on his mind.

Redeem from what? Some would say,
Our debt of sin He would pay.
To trade his life for our penalty of sin,
Giving us new hope beginning with Him.

Lora Brand

Religious Christmas 3

What is this Christmas all about,
Who gives reason for all to shout,
It began long ago with the birth of a boy,
For all mankind to give them joy.

Birthday celebrations this season it will be,
As a king was born for man to see.
Gifts were given on that special day,
To a baby born in a manger of hay.

This baby born to see mankind free,
Of sin and death throughout all history.
Jesus, his name, lifted high and above,
Demonstrating to us all of God's love.

Together let's celebrate this festive season,
For now you know the very reason.
Not just about gifts, holidays and fun,
But to remember and honour God's only true son.

So spread the love and give Christmas cheer,
Drawing many around and keeping them near.

Lora Brand

Religious Christmas 4

A season to be jolly, they say,
For Christmas is no ordinary day,
A time to remember what this is all about,
Let's give Jesus a praise and a shout!

Lora Brand

Religious Christmas 5

Christmas unveils a master plan,
Of God himself in the form of a man.
Born to be the King of Kings,
To be Lord and ruler of all things.

How did this start? Where did it begin?
'Twas a plan to redeem man's plight of sin.
Beginning with Adam and Eve – they ate that fruit,
An act of rebellion there is no dispute.

Now hiding from God – naked and ashamed,
On the serpent, their actions soon were blamed.
Broken fellowship their disobedience then caused,
Unity between God and man now paused.

But God in His love devised a way,
As unity with Him is set to stay.
Redemption must come in order for this –
An action of exchange – a debt not amiss.

Redeem from what? Some would say,
Our debt of wrongs He would pay,
To trade His life for our penalty of sin,
Giving new hope beginning with Him.

How is this possible? One would ask,
Sacrificing a life for this very task!
Given upon the alter His blood and His flesh,
Atoning our souls – new life afresh.

Red for redemption at Christmas to remember,
The life given for our surrender.
The penalty of sin pardoned through love,

Restoring us back to the Father above.

'R' to Restore man's heart back to Him,
To seek His face and surrender the sin.
No shame! No guilt! To come between,
His love for you can now be seen.

'E' for Eternity, life beyond the grave,
An eternal gift to you He gave.
Heaven-bound to live forever,
As kings and priests, no more sorrow ever.

'D' for Death as Jesus went to the cross,
Trading a life for a life – there is no loss.
The ultimate price for love He paid,
Breathing His last for you, His life He laid.

Then to rise and say, 'It is finished,
The enemy's plan is now diminished.'

Lora Brand

Religious Christmas 6

My Christmas gift I have prepared for you,
Not gold nor silver just to name two.
Far greater than money could ever buy,
My life for you an endless supply
Comes with no cost but everything to gain,
One that will last and always remain.
My love is what I have for you,
To last a lifetime and carry you through.
Good times and bad, all seasons you live,
Here is my gift, to you I give.

Lora Brand

Religious Christmas encouragement 1

Christmas a hard time for some, I know,
Very difficult to have that season's glow,
A time that reminds of heartfelt pain,
Reliving that moment over again.

Not all is lost as this time draws near,
As I send you love and Christmas cheer.
May you be surrounded with those who care,
Warmth and love, this Christmas, they will share.

My prayer is for a new hope to begin,
To stir in your heart fresh life again,
For you to dare to dream new dreams,
Not simply seeing life just as it seems.

Thinking of you at this Christmas season,
As life often does not give reason,
But I know this one very thing –
It is the blessings Jesus can bring.

Lora Brand

Religious Christmas poem to encourage the heart 2

Yet you desired faithfulness even in the womb;
you taught me wisdom in that secret place
Psalms 51:6 (NIV)

Wisdom is something we should desire,
A quality that we can all acquire.
With wisdom comes truth and facing some things,
The difficult times that life sometimes brings.
See things as they truly are,
And your life will flourish and continue far.
Dare to face the truth ahead,
For there's One who'll walk with you, as He said.
For He was born one Christmas night,
And for you He will stand and fight.
So let Him into your heart right now,
As He will strengthen you, and show you how –
To live a life that is truly blessed,
For you can trust that He knows best.

Lora Brand

Religious Christmas poem to encourage the heart 3

But one thing I do: Forgetting what is
behind and straining toward what is ahead,
I press on toward the goal to win the prize for which
God has called me heavenward in Christ Jesus.
Philippians 3:13-14 (NIV)

How do we let go of what lies behind?
Making the path of our future blind.
How can I see what may lie ahead?
Still there are tears not yet shed.
From a life that has sorrow and regret,
How is it possible to simply forget?

I am the way, the truth and life, said He.
Jesus is that way; He is the key.
So, this Christmas, remember this one thing,
And allow next year good things to bring.

Lora Brand

Religious Christmas poem to encourage the heart 4

'For I know the plans I have for you,'
declares the Lord, 'plans to prosper you
and not to harm you,
plans to give you hope and a future.'
Jeremiah 29:11 (NIV)

Do not let the past dictate your future,
Making you think you are a failure.
Leave the past where it belongs,
And in your heart begin new songs.
Change what you can as best you know how,
Full steam ahead, with hand to the plough.
In order to go on you must let go,
And may encouragement come from friends you know.
There is one friend who believes in you,
Who can help you start your life anew.
At Christmas many people celebrate His birth,
Not really knowing why He came to earth.
Why He came – 'twas for you and for me,
To give us a future that we can see.

Lora Brand

Religious Christmas poem to encourage the heart 5

Never will I leave you;
never will I forsake you.
Hebrews 13:5 (NIV)

Have you ever felt you've been left by yourself,
Like some old grocery line on a supermarket shelf,
To be disappointed with so many things,
That living life sometimes brings.
Well, there is a Man that you can trust,
Who will never throw you out like dirt or dust.
He'll stick to you closer than a brother,
And nurture you like a true mother.
So, thank Him today as Christmas draws nigh,
Letting light and hope replace your sigh.
For He will never let you down,
And to Him you are worthy of a crown.

Lora Brand

Religious Christmas poem to encourage the heart 6

But seek first his kingdom and his righteousness,
and all these things will be given to you as well.
Matthew 6:33 (NIV)

There are so many things we put first in our life,
Often causing us sorrow and strife.
Decisions we've made, not always the best,
In search of love and peace, our personal quest.
Those things we can have! And more to gain,
Be poured on us like refreshing rain.
If only we seek first His ways to live,
There is so much more He will freely give.
He knows what will hurt us and bring us to shame,
So, call on Him for there's power in His name.
There is more to His kingdom than Christmas cheer,
Much greater than just 'time for a beer'.
So, I hope you will find all His treasure,
For to give you much, is His pleasure.

Lora Brand

Religious Christmas poem to encourage the heart 7

Turn from evil and do good;
seek peace and pursue it.
Psalms 34:14 (NIV)

To desire after peace is a treasure to behold,
A free gift, cannot be bought or sold.
Surpasses all understanding of situations you face,
Putting your mind at ease, in a comfortable place.
A heart that is still and has a knowing within,
Able to face life with a smile and a grin.
This was made possible through Jesus's birth,
Bringing peace and love to men on earth.

Lora Brand

Religious Christmas poem to encourage the heart 8

There is a time for everything,
and a season for every activity under the heavens.
Ecclesiastes 3:1 (NIV)

Seasons come and seasons go –
How long they last, we do not know.
Where you are right now will pass away,
For ahead will be a better day.
Walk through this chapter, but don't be alone,
Dial up Jesus on your personal phone.
Talk to him about your life at hand,
He will give you strength and help you stand.
His purpose for you will begin to unfold,
Releasing you from this interval's hold.
Jesus was born for this very reason,
That's why we celebrate this Christmas season.

Lora Brand

Religious Christmas poem to encourage the heart 9

Love never fails.
1 Corinthians 13:8 (NIV)

There is a love that is always true,
One you can trust your whole life through.
Does not matter the condition of your heart,
Has always loved you from the very start.
Let no guilt or shame hold you bound,
For in His love freedom is found.
This Christmas, may you be touched by His love,
A gift for you given from above.
Take heart today in all you do,
And allow His love to carry you through.

Lora Brand

Religious Christmas poem to encourage the heart 10

For he will command his angels concerning you
to guard you in all your ways.
Psalms 91:11 (NIV)

There are times in our life when we feel alone,
Disappointments and loss, our hearts will groan.
A difficult task to walk the way one should go,
How to continue, we do not always know.
There is a promise for you in your life,
That He will watch over you in all your strife.
His Angels watch over you, always ready to defend,
Preserving the goodness in you to the end.
This Christmas remember He is *for* you,
And is always there to help you through.

Lora Brand

Religious Christmas poem to encourage the heart
11

May the God of hope fill you with all
joy and peace as you trust in him,
so that you may overflow with hope
by the power of the Holy Spirit. Romans 15:13 (NIV)

Misery comes when we have no hope,
Making it difficult with life to cope.
There is a joy – can be given to you,
Making each day fresh and new.
This joy brings peace to your heart and soul,
Healing the wounds and making you whole.
Come to Him who gives you this joy,
Celebrating Christmas, the birth of this boy –
Who then grew up to become a King,
For freedom and joy in your life to bring.
Believe in Him and surrender your all,
Don't be mistaken – it's you – He did call.

Lora Brand

Religious Christmas poem to encourage the heart 12

Therefore I tell you, do not worry about your life,
what you will eat; or about your body, what you will wear.
For life is more than food, and the body more than clothes.
Luke 12:22-23 (NIV)

Is your heart sad, or anxious or full of fears?
Are you weary from crying so many tears?
Life at times is difficult to grasp.
Sometimes it seems too hard a task.
There is One who offers to make your burdens light,
If you're only willing to surrender the fight.
To cast all your cares upon His name,
Truly you will never be the same.
Christmas is a time for goodwill and cheer,
The secret to that is to draw Him near,
To allow Him into that secret place,
To see Him as He is, face to face.

Lora Brand

Religious Christmas poem to encourage the heart
13

A furious squall came up, and the waves
broke over the boat, so that it was nearly swamped.
Jesus was in the stern, sleeping on a cushion.
The disciples woke him and said to him,
'Teacher, don't you care if we drown?'
Mark 4:37-38 (NIV)

Sometimes it feels that He is asleep,
As we drown in our sorrows and troubles deep.
Where is our help in times of despair?
Can He not, see? Or does He not care?
This is when we need to believe,
To surrender all and simply receive –
His loving arms and outstretched hands,
To calm the storm at His command.
This we call faith, trusting in One we cannot see,
Surrendering it all to let it be.
Our Christmas tells the birth of Jesus that day,
Then to die for you, His price to pay.
Abundant life for you to gain,
Else His life was taken in vain.

Lora Brand

Sympathy 1

There are no words that I could say,
To ease the pain of what you face today.
The darkest days, seems there's no tomorrow,
As filled with sadness and much sorrow.

Thinking of you at this time right now,
For life continues, but you cannot see how.
The days ahead filled with grief and pain,
Till the day where you will smile again.

Life often dishes a very tough blow,
Why? Is the question no one will know.
To accept this loss, a tough path to take,
Laying no blame is the stand to make.

Life happens and it isn't always fair,
For some it is often too much to bear.
Let those around you comfort your heart,
Drawing together, not drifting apart.

Allow yourself to grieve how you need,
However long it takes is acceptable indeed.
To mourn the loss of one so close to your soul,
Will take time before you begin to feel whole.

Be encouraged to take each day as it may come,
Expecting little, at times might feel numb.
But to find a place of solace and still,
Where out of your mouth your heart can spill.

All the thoughts and turmoil within,
This is where your healing may truly begin.
I send you all my love and heartfelt care,
As you walk through this valley of deep despair.

Sympathy 2

Thoughts of you
today I send,
As a season in life
has come to an end.
To experience loss
there are no words to say,
May you find strength
day by day.
To walk this journey
of sadness of heart,
I pray time heals
as new days start.

Lora Brand

Religious sympathy 1

I see you pass by and give a beautiful smile,
Yet hidden behind those eyes lies something deep.
All's fine when busy, no room to stop awhile,
Nights often lonely and without sleep.

To suffer loss leaves a hole in one's heart,
Seemingly broken beyond all repair.
How to go on and make that new start?
Does not seem right nor does it seem fair.

To live life is often a risk and a gamble,
Not always fulfilling all our hopes and dreams.
Treasure to find is a way through the shamble,
Finding new hope not as impossible as it seems.

Grief goes deep into one's soul,
How long it lasts I dare not guess.
When again will you ever feel whole?
That I cannot answer I must confess.

I know one thing only time will tell,
You will laugh, smile and dream again.
You and others will see you now are well,
As the sting decreases from your loss and pain.

Stick close to those who love and care,
Giving shoulder to cry on and outstretched hand.
Allow them to carry that burden you bear,
As together with you they will stand.

In those lonely moments He will guide you through,
That your heart be mended, no longer sad.
With peace in your thoughts as your day breaks new,
Leaving cherished memories of life once had.

Lora Brand

Religious sympathy 2 (suicide)

Tragedy has come and struck your heart,
Shooting arrows like fiery darts.
The loss you carry all too much to bear,
Just isn't right, nor is it fair.

To have one you love taken from you,
As a mind was masked with a clouded view,
To believe that life has no more to gain,
Therefore, no wish on this earth to remain.

A liar, a thief, the enemy has come,
With trickery and a trap, making one numb,
To blind the eye of a future to see,
In making one believe, *there is nothing for me*.

The plan of the enemy is to destroy one's soul,
Crippling the mind with an unshakable hold.
Even in this, God's plan is not finished,
For His power and authority never is diminished.

Where the enemy has gained some final ground,
Eternal life in Him can still be found,
As the heart of one is only known to Him,
Judging no confusion as the light grew dim.

He sees beyond a mind, tormented and withered,
Through storms of life beaten and weathered.
He sees beyond a heart, that's shaken and torn,
Leaving one lost and completely forlorn.

Trust in Him those things you cannot comprehend,
As time will come and your heart will mend.
Shout, grieve, cry – let it out best,

Till your mind at last can come to some rest.

The plans of His you cannot know,
Surrendering this mess is the way to go.
Releasing what you cannot understand,
Though you grieve, dare to take His leading hand.

No sense this makes as you come to Him,
A choice of courage mustered from within.
To give to Him all that is lost,
Trusting that Jesus paid the cost.

Under His shadow is the place to hide,
A shattered heart empty inside.
Time is the essence to heal that heart,
One day at a time is where you start.

Tell Him all, just as it is,
Making your burden not yours, but His.

Lora Brand

9 781763 786455